# Refugees & Asylum Seekers

DAVE DALTON

www.heinemann.co.uk/library
Visit our website to find out more information about Heinemann Library books.

To order:

 Phone 44 (0) 1865 888066

 Send a fax to 44 (0) 1865 314091

 Visit the Heinemann Bookshop at www.heinemann.co.uk/library to browse our catalogue and order online.

First published in Great Britain by Heinemann Library, Halley Court, Jordan Hill, Oxford OX2 8EJ, part of Harcourt Education.
Heinemann is a registered trademark of Harcourt Education Ltd.

Editorial: Jilly Attwood and Kathy Peltan
Design: Ron Kamen and Celia Jones
Illustrations: Jeff Edwards
Picture Research: Ruth Blair and Kay Altwegg
Production: Séverine Ribierre

Originated by Modern Age

Printed and bound in China by South China Printing Company

The paper used to print this book comes from sustainable resources.
10 digit ISBN 0 431 01385 3 (hardback)
13 digit ISBN 978 0 431 01385 5 (hardback)
10 09 08 07 06
10 9 8 7 6 5 4 3 2 1
10 digit ISBN 0 431 01389 6 (paperback)
13 digit ISBN 978 0 431 01389 3 (paperback)
11 10 09 08 07
10 9 8 7 6 5 4 3 2 1

British Library Cataloguing in Publication Data

Dalton, Dave
Refugees and Asylum Seekers
(People on the Move)
305.9'06914

A full catalogue record for this book is available from the British Library.

Acknowledgements
The publishers would like to thank the following for permission to reproduce photographs:
Corbis pp.11(Chris Rainier), p.21(Robert Patrick), p.27(Dave Bartruff), p.30(Bettmann), p.34(Anthony Njuguna/Reuters) p.40(Najlah Feanny), p.42(J.B.Russell), p.43(Steve Starr): Dave Dalton pp.29(t), 38, 45; Getty Images/Hulton Archive pp.9, 19, 31, 33; Mary Evans Picture Library p.17; Oxfam Archive(Alan Leather) p.7; Panos Pictures pp. 36, 41, p.5(Martin Adler), pp.4, 8, 13(Crispin Hughes), p.15(Jon Spall), p.23(Jeroen Oerlemans), p.25(Andrew Testa), p.29(b)(Howard Davies).

Cover photograph of a man carrying his father on his back as they flee conflict in Monrovia, Liberia, reproduced with permission of Panos(Martin Adler).

The publishers would like to thank Angus Willson, Director, Worldaware for his assistance in the preparation of this book.

Every effort has been made to contact copyright holders of any material reproduced in this book. Any omissions will be rectified in subsequent printings if notice is given to the publishers.

Disclaimer
All the Internet addresses (URLs) given in this book were valid at the time of going to press. However, due to the dynamic nature of the Internet, some addresses may have changed, or sites may have changed or ceased to exist since publication. While the author and Publishers regret any inconvenience this may cause readers, no responsibility for any such changes can be accepted by either author or the Publishers.

# Contents

Words in bold, **like this,** are explained in the glossary.

# Introduction

## Fear makes people move

When we talk about people on the move we usually mean **migrants**. Migrants move from one place to another, and usually settle down permanently. But this book is about people who move because things are so bad where they live that they will go anywhere to get away. They may escape taking only what they can carry. What could make them just flee, leaving everything behind?

## Clemente

Clemente Chico is a **displaced person**. He was forced to leave his home in Ungundu in Angola, Africa because of the civil war between the government and a rebel army. In 2000 he was living in Ungundu Camp, Kuito.

"I have a wife – Augusta Chemba – and five children aged from eleven years to four months. We came from Ungundu, 60 kilometres [37 miles] away, and it took us three days to walk here [Kuito]. The rebel soldiers arrived after dark – we heard running, and shots. They started burning houses. I saw our house burning. I took the eleven-year-old and the four-year-old. I shoulder-carried the little one. Augusta took the baby, of course, and the six year-old. The middle child, the nine-year-old, went with another family. We spent two nights on the way here ... At Lungundwa we slept in the school – and that's where we all met up, that's where we realized that we had all survived ... I brought a tool for cutting wood. I carried loads for other people, to earn money to pay for food. When I was carrying loads, the eleven-year-old had to carry the four-year-old."

Clemente

## Consider this:
### survivors

We know about the difficulties and sufferings of refugees because we can talk to the survivors, who escaped. But many of the survivors left behind friends and family who did not escape.

## Amuh

Amuh is a member of the Karen people from Myanmar (formerly called Burma). She fled her home and lives in a refugee camp in Thailand. The Karen people are fighting for independence from Myanmar. The government treats them brutally.

"I lived with my family in a village called Kawmura in Burma. In April 1984 the government forces came and fired shells into the village. We had to flee. My husband was away, he was a fighter with the independence forces. I had two young children – the youngest was six months old. I carried the baby on my back, and the toddler walked. I had a basket with some clothes, cooking pots, and blankets.

"The village leader arranged with the Thai authorities for us to move to this camp. We get a food ration from a charity. People earn money by working for farmers. Now I earn a living by weaving."

Amuh

## Isa

Isa Bakthari is an **asylum seeker** from Afghanistan. He was interviewed in the UK in 2000.

"The fighting has been going on in my country for years. When I was fourteen a bomb blew up close to me and threw me into the air. My arm and leg were broken. Then a bomb killed my father, mother, and little sister. I came home from school and saw what had happened. I can't go back to Afghanistan – please, no – there is fighting, fighting all the time."

Isa

In Afghanistan in 2001, women and children fled from the latest fighting in a war between the government and rebel forces that had started in 1979. Refugees from the war fled to Iran and Pakistan, and from place to place within Afghanistan.

# Forced to flee

Every year, millions of people are forced to flee their homes because of war and **persecution**. Governments have a duty to protect these people.

## War and refugees

When people cross a border to escape war, they become refugees. If they flee within their own country, they are known as **internally displaced people**. In this book we will use the word refugee for both groups of people.

## Persecution and asylum seekers

Persecution can take the form of arrest, torture, imprisonment, assassination, or massacre, because of a person's religion, race, or beliefs. When people flee from persecution they are known as **asylum seekers**. Asylum means safety under the protection of a government.

Refugees and asylum seekers want safety, above all. They have left behind their homes, livelihoods, and possessions. They need food, clothing, shelter, health care, and schools for their children. They may stay in their new homes, find work and learn the language. They become **immigrants**. But they may be waiting until it is safe to return home. The wait may be many years.

## Human rights

The safety, food, shelter, health care, and education that refugees and asylum seekers want and need are **human rights**. The **United Nations** (UN) is an international organization that was set up in 1945 to keep peace between nations. The UN's Universal Declaration of Human Rights, adopted in 1948, lists the rights that all member states should respect and defend.

Article 14 is about asylum: "Everyone has the right to seek and enjoy in other countries asylum from persecution." Many of the other Articles are about **civil rights**. They include:
- equality between the sexes and races
- fair criminal trials
- the right to vote and to join political parties and trade unions
- freedom from torture or cruel, inhuman, or degrading treatment or punishment
- freedom of religious belief.

To sum up in the words of Article 3: "Everyone has the right to life, liberty, and security of person." Attacks on these rights, or on people trying to claim these rights, are what asylum seekers are fleeing from.

When war broke out in Bangladesh in 1971, nine million refugees fled over the border into India. See page 19.

## The rights of refugees

The UN set up the Office of the **United Nations High Commissioner for Refugees (UNHCR)** in 1950, to protect refugees and resolve refugee problems worldwide. Since then it has helped 50 million people to restart their lives. It is now helping over 17 million people. It aims to help them to return home when it is safe to do so. If they can never return home, it helps them settle in another country. Meanwhile it houses them in refugee camps.

The 1951 Geneva **Convention** defined the rights of refugees. It defined a refugee as "A person who is outside his/her country of nationality or habitual residence; has a well-founded fear of persecution because of his/her race, religion, nationality, membership in a particular social group or political opinion; and is unable or unwilling ... to return there, for fear of persecution."

Strangely, this looks more like a definition of an asylum seeker. It is the basis on which people claim asylum, and governments decide whether to admit them. The UNHCR, however, looks after refugees from war, including many internally displaced people. Governments also have duties to refugees under the Geneva Convention. There are also international development agencies and local community-based organizations that help refugees.

# chapter two

# War

## Civilian casualties

A battlefield is a dangerous place for soldiers. It is even more dangerous for civilians.

### Caught in the crossfire

Traditionally, wars are fought between armies in uniforms. But civilians cannot always get out of the way, particularly if the fighting is in a city. Modern weapons, such as missiles, may hurt nearby civilians, even if they are aimed at military targets.

In the urgency of war, armies **requisition** buildings and food. Villages, towns, and fields of crops become battlefields. Homeless, hungry, frightened people flee for safety. Everything collapses: transport, water and food supplies, health care, and law and order. People may escape to safety, but still not have food, shelter, or other necessities. This happened in the Democratic Republic of Congo (formerly known as Zaire). People fled from fighting into the nearby forests. Up to 3.5 million people died from hunger and disease, between 1994 and 2004.

Nevertheless, international law says that armies must avoid harming civilians, and refugees from the fighting should be protected. They should expect especially good treatment if they flee within their own country. But refugees are not always treated well.

When fighting reached the city of Kuito in Angola in 1993, a stray shell hit the home of Gloria Alegria, who was then eight. Three of her brothers were killed. Gloria lost the sight of one eye, and is paralysed in one leg.

### Targeting civilians

Sometimes the armed forces deliberately target civilians. During World War II (1939–1945), both sides bombed cities to destroy the **economy** and the morale of their enemy. Germany bombed Britain, killing 60,000 people and injuring another 235,000. British and US air forces bombed Germany. In Hamburg 50,000 people were killed, in Dresden up to 150,000 were killed, many of them refugees. The Americans bombed Japan between

## Leaving the cities

Fearing the effects of bombing during World War II, the British government organized the **evacuation** of 1.75 million people from cities. They especially wanted young children with their mothers, pregnant women, and disabled people to evacuate. Another two million people moved themselves.

These children are being evacuated from London to the countryside, during World War II.

1941 and 1945. In a single air raid on Tokyo there were 125,000 casualties, 40 per cent of the city was destroyed, and one million people were made homeless. The atomic bomb dropped by the USA on the city of Hiroshima killed 70,000 people, injured 51,000, and destroyed 70,000 buildings.

## Eastern Europe

In the same war, Germany fought the Soviet Union over a huge area of eastern Europe and western Russia. Both armies deliberately destroyed crops, buildings, and bridges as they retreated, so as to leave nothing for the other side. Civilians were left with no food or shelter, in a country with harsh winters. By the end of the war, 17,000 towns and settlements, and over 70,000 villages, were completely or partly destroyed in the Soviet Union. Up to 19 million civilians died. Millions more fled from the fighting and destruction.

## Consider this: no escape

When air forces bomb entire cities, and ruthless armies fight with modern weapons, civilian casualties are bound to be high. Sixty-five per cent of the deaths in World War II were of civilians.

# Revolution, rebellion, and civil war

Life becomes even more risky for civilians if they are caught up in a revolution, rebellion, or civil war. In a revolution, one group of people takes over the government from another, often with some violence. In a rebellion, large numbers of people take up arms against the government. And in a civil war, two sides fight for the control of their country.

## Dangerous passions

In most revolutions, and many civil wars, there are deep differences in beliefs between the two sides. The soldiers are not merely obeying the orders of their officers, they believe in the cause they are fighting for. They may feel that the enemy is not just an army to be defeated, but a hated class, political party, or category of people, to be destroyed. To capture a town is not just a step towards conquering the country, but an opportunity to kill the local leaders of the opposition. The distinction between soldiers and civilians becomes blurred, and people cannot hope just to try to keep out of the crossfire. If their side loses, they must all flee, or risk massacres and other **atrocities**.

In 1793 the Vendée district of France revolted against the country's revolutionary government. The government's response was merciless. Their general reported: "I have trampled their children beneath our horses' feet; I have massacred their women, so they will no longer give birth to brigands (thieves). I do not have a single prisoner to reproach me. I have exterminated them all... Mercy is not a revolutionary sentiment."

## Soldiers and supporters

The soldiers of rebellions, revolutions, and resistance movements often use **guerrilla** methods. They do not wear uniforms, and make quick raids on government forces, disappearing back into the forests, fields, and villages. The local people may support the fighters, or may be unable to avoid them. The forces trying to capture or defeat the guerrillas have a difficult problem. They cannot fight an enemy they cannot find.

## Consider this:
### victors and victims

Many of the conflicts in the world today are civil wars, revolts, and rebellions. They all affect civilians. They may even target civilians. In recent conflicts, civilian casualties have been as high as 84 per cent of the total number.

# Attacking authority

Rebels usually want the support of the people. But sometimes the civilians are at risk from attacks by the rebels. The rebels' strategy is to attack the government by attacking the people. This is likely to stretch the government forces trying to protect the people, or to show the government's weakness by its inability to protect the people. Either way, it suits the rebels. If people flee from the attacks into refugee camps, they become the responsibility of the government. This adds to the pressure on the government.

Often the government forces are tempted to treat all civilians as either fighters, or supporters of the fighters. The result is indiscriminate attacks on the civilian population. If the conflict happens at the same time as a drought, the government may not help the famine victims in rebellious areas. Charities may not be able to get food to the hungry people, because of the fighting.

Children gather at a refugee camp in Ethiopia during the famine of 1984–1985. The famine affected 150 million inhabitants of sub-Saharan Africa.

*case study:*

# The Angolan civil war

Angola is one of many African countries that have suffered years of civil war. Millions of people have been **displaced** from their homes by the conflict.

This map shows Angola and the towns mentioned in the text.

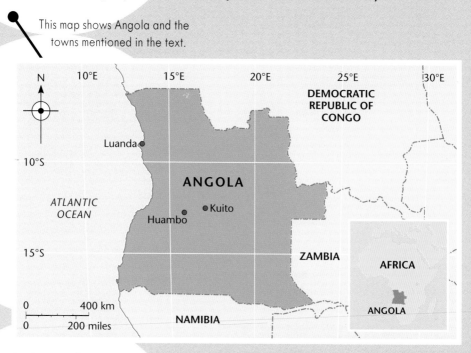

## Independence and war

Angola remained a **colony** of Portugal long after other colonial powers gave independence to their African countries. There were two political parties, called UNITA and MPLA, seeking independence for Angola. Portugal gave the country independence suddenly in 1975, and MPLA formed the government. Almost immediately, conflict broke out between the MPLA government and UNITA, which also wanted power. Other countries quickly became involved. Cuba and the Soviet Union helped the MPLA. The USA and South Africa helped UNITA. The war dragged on, with a peace process that broke down twice when UNITA refused to accept the results of elections. Finally, government troops killed the leader of UNITA, and the war ended in 2002.

## Death and destruction

Hundreds of thousands of people died during the 27 years of war. Civilians in towns died, as well as troops. People also died of hunger, because the fighting made farming impossible and stopped food aid reaching those who needed it. Both sides laid thousands of **anti-personnel mines** to protect themselves, but when the fighting moved away, the mines injured civilians. Houses, hospitals, roads, and railways were destroyed, and many thousands of people became refugees.

# Luanda

Many refugees found their way to the capital city, Luanda. Here they set up permanent homes, and found jobs. Luanda today has many street-children, orphaned or separated from their parents by the war. They live by begging or doing odd jobs.

Rodrina Faustina tells how the war affected her and her family.

"I am 42, married, with six children. My son Faustino lost his leg when he stepped on a mine when he was twelve. We lived in Katabola village, but we had to leave last September because UNITA attacked the village . . . We walked here, it's about 50 kilometres [31 miles], and it took us three days. At first we were put in schools in Kuito, then we came to this camp. This wasn't the first time UNITA had attacked. In October 1990 they came to the village, stealing things. I tried to escape but they shot me in the leg. I got first aid, then I was brought to the hospital here in Kuito and they had to amputate my leg below the knee."

Rodrina

## Refugee camps

The city of Kuito, in the central highlands, was held by government forces. It was a magnet for refugees from villages attacked by UNITA forces. They walked there, sometimes for many days, bringing with them only what they could carry. In the camp they relied on food aid provided by the World Food Programme. The food had to be flown in to Kuito, because the road was not safe. The Red Cross organized a monthly distribution of maize, beans, oil, salt, and soap. Some refugees grew a few vegetables on tiny plots of land next to their shelters. Many gathered firewood to earn a few pennies. International charities provided other help. For example they drilled tube-wells to provide clean water, built latrines for hygienic **sanitation**, and provided extra food for **malnourished** children.

Rosa Kandeya grew cabbages by the railway tracks in Kaala, near Huambo. All the refugees were vulnerable to illness, because they were badly fed and crowded together into a disused railway station.

# Expulsion

Refugees hope to return home eventually. But sometimes, during or after wars, governments expel people. Millions of people are forced to move, with little hope of returning home.

## Moving the borders

Wars often change borders, as the winning country takes over territory from the loser. People find they are citizens of a different country. They have to adapt to the laws, and perhaps the official language, of the country in which they now live.

## Moving the people

Sometimes the powers which impose the new borders also make the people move. At the end of World War II, the border between the Soviet Union and Poland moved up to 322 kilometres (200 miles) west. The border between Poland and Germany also moved west. Millions of Germans living on the Polish side of the border were forced to leave and find new homes in Germany. At the same time, Czechoslovakia expelled 3.5 million ethnic Germans from the Sudetenland. This is the area on the border between the two countries. Germany had taken over the Sudetenland in 1938, but Czechoslovakia recovered it in 1945. There were other expulsions: Italians from Yugoslavia, and Turks from Bulgaria and Greece. Altogether there were 12 million **displaced** people in Europe at the end of World War II. Some were anxious to return to their home, but others were unable or unwilling to go back.

This map shows the areas from which German people had to move at the end of World War II.

N 50°N
5°E
North Sea

DENMARK
10°E

Baltic Sea
15°E
20°E

NETHERLANDS

BELGIUM

45°N

LUXEMBOURG

FRANCE

GERMANY

POLAND

CZECHOSLOVAKIA

AUSTRIA

SWITZERLAND

-·—·— Germany pre-1945

     Sudetenland

     Areas which Germany lost in 194

0     200 km

0     150 miles

## Consider this:
### stay or return?

Some people expelled from their homelands settle down in their destination. Others wait, perhaps for a long time, to return home. As we will see later, it depends on how well they are treated in their new homes.

The Shatila camp in Lebanon houses refugees from Palestine.

## Taking the land

The victors sometimes move the defeated people so they can take their land. The government of the USA took land from the Native Americans, sometimes by treaty, sometimes by conquest. Sixty-thousand Native Americans were moved from Georgia to Oklahoma in the winter of 1831–1832. Many died on the journey. Later, as settlers moved into the Great Plains between the Mississippi and the Rocky Mountains, the Native Americans were moved to **reservations**, usually on the worst land.

## Arabs and Israelis

In 1948, Jewish settlers in the British-governed territory of Palestine declared an independent state of Israel. The surrounding Arab countries felt that the Arab-speaking Palestinian people should run Palestine. They attacked, but Israel survived. Many Palestinian Arabs fled the fighting, and others were expelled. They went to refugee camps in the Gaza Strip, between Israel and Egypt, and in the neighbouring countries of Lebanon and Jordan. Altogether there were 982,000 refugees. Jewish **immigrants** continued to arrive in Israel, creating settlements on land that had belonged to Arabs. But not all the Arabs were expelled from Israel. Some of the refugee camps set up in 1948 are still there today. Generations have grown up waiting for the right to return to their land in Palestine.

# Chapter three

# Persecution

## Religious persecution

Sometimes believers in one religion or **sect persecute** believers in another religion or sect. The persecuted people may **migrate** to escape this persecution.

### Christians and others

In the **Middle Ages** there were Jewish communities all over Christian Europe. They were usually tolerated, although confined to **ghettoes**. But there were occasional expulsions and massacres. In 1492, Spain offered its Jewish people a choice: to convert to Christianity, or leave the country. About 20,000 families chose to leave. In 1502, Spain's Muslims were given the same choice.

This map shows some of the migrations caused by religious persecution. Jews and Muslims left Spain for the Ottoman Empire.

## Consider this: who benefits?

When people migrated to escape religious persecution, they gained the freedom to believe what they wanted. The countries that made them welcome also gained. The migrants were determined to succeed, and their growing prosperity helped to make their new homeland prosperous.

### Heretics

There are many versions of Christian faith. In the past, the leaders of the established church would define all other versions as heresy. This means incorrect and sinful beliefs. In 1520, a priest in Germany called Martin Luther broke away from the Catholic Church. This was the beginning of Protestantism. Another influential religious leader, Jean Calvin, founded another branch of Protestantism in 1541. Followers of Luther were called Lutherans, and followers of Calvin were called Calvinists. For the next 150 years Europe, especially Germany and France, was torn by religious wars. People had three choices: convert to the majority religion; suffer persecution and possibly death for their faith; or flee for safety.

## Exile

In Catholic France, the Calvinists were known as Huguenots. In 1572, 20,000 Huguenots were massacred in France. In 1598, the king of France finally granted toleration to the Huguenots. When that toleration was removed, in 1685, up to 400,000 Huguenots left France. Most of them moved to England. Many were skilled craft workers, so their move was a great loss for France and a gain for England.

## Migration

England became a Protestant country. Catholics, and members of minority Protestant sects, such as the Puritans, were put in prison for their beliefs. In 1620, the first Puritan pilgrims left England and crossed the Atlantic Ocean in a ship called the *Mayflower*. They settled in Massachusetts, in what is now the USA. Soon 20,000 more joined them. Further **colonies** on the east coast of the USA were founded by other religious minorities. The Quakers settled in Pennsylvania, which then attracted religious exiles from Germany. Catholics settled in Maryland.

In 1620, 102 Protestants sailed from Plymouth, England, in the *Mayflower*. Thirty-five of them were Puritans. Both groups were fleeing religious persecution in England.

case study:

# The partition of India, 1947

The Indian **sub-continent** is the region made up of India, Pakistan, Sri Lanka, and Bangladesh. It has many different religions, and a tragic history of intolerance and violence.

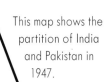

This map shows the partition of India and Pakistan in 1947.

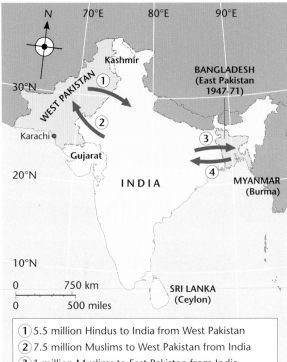

① 5.5 million Hindus to India from West Pakistan
② 7.5 million Muslims to West Pakistan from India
③ 1 million Muslims to East Pakistan from India
④ 3.3 million Hindus to India from East Pakistan

## Hindus and Muslims

Originally, all the people of the sub-continent were Hindus, apart from the Buddhists in Sri Lanka and Nepal. Islam arrived in the 8th century, and by the 13th century it was the majority religion in the north. In many places, Hindus and Muslims lived together and tolerated each other.

## British rule

In the 18th century, the British conquered the sub-continent and ruled it as a single **colony**. Some Indians became Christians. In 1945 Britain prepared to give India its independence. The Muslims were afraid they would be the minority in a single Indian state with a big Hindu majority. Their political party, the Muslim League, persuaded the British government to create a separate country for the Muslims. This was in the two regions that became East and West Pakistan.

Muslim women boarding a train at New Delhi in India, to reach the safety of newly independent Pakistan in 1947.

## Partition

After independence on 15 August 1947, there were still millions of Hindus in Pakistan and millions of Muslims in India. Soon two huge floods of religious refugees poured across the new borders. From West Pakistan 5.5 million Hindus entered India, while 7.5 million Muslims moved in the other direction into Pakistan. One million Muslims crossed into East Pakistan, and 3.3 million Hindus left. Altogether, over 17 million people lost their homes, livelihoods, and possessions. Half a million people died in violence between Muslims and Hindus during the chaos of partition.

## Violence

Since 1947, there has been an uneasy peace between India and Pakistan, and between the different religions in each country. There have been occasional outbreaks of conflict. In 1992, violence erupted after Hindu extremists demolished the Muslim mosque at Ayodhya. In 2002 more than 1000 people, mainly Muslims, died in riots in Gujarat, after an attack on a train full of Hindu pilgrims.

In 1971, the people of East Pakistan demanded independence. The movement was violently repressed by the army of Pakistan. India intervened to help the independence movement, and East Pakistan became the independent state of Bangladesh.

Bangladesh and Pakistan have Muslims from both the **sects** of Islam: the Sunni and Shia. Some members of the Sunni majority in Pakistan have become increasingly violent against the Shia minority, and also against Christians. In May 2004, a Sunni extremist killed 15 people and injured 125 in a crowded Shia mosque in Karachi.

# Racial persecution

People of different races, speaking different languages and with different religions, can and should live together in peace. But whenever a minority is **persecuted** by the majority, members of the minority will migrate to escape the persecution.

## Jewish persecution

Jewish communities in Europe were persecuted from medieval times. Even when their faith was tolerated, they were not given the same rights as all other citizens. This was not achieved in Britain until 1871, and in Italy until 1945. The position of Jews was worst in Russia. There was a big Jewish population there, in an area now covered by Poland and the Ukraine. They were a distinctive race, with a distinctive appearance, culture, religion, and language. It was easy to blame them for any difficulties. The ruling class linked Jews with dangerous revolutionary ideas. Organized attacks on the Jews started in Russia in 1881, and the government did nothing to prevent them. A second wave of attacks occurred in 1903–1906. The Jews emigrated in huge numbers. Between 1881 and 1914, 150,000 Jews migrated to Britain. Between 1900 and 1914 over 1,500,000 Jews migrated to the USA.

## A Jewish homeland

Some Jews felt that the real problem was that they did not have a country of their own, and that they should return to their original homeland in Palestine. After Palestine came under British control in 1918, Jews began to migrate there. More moved when the **anti-Semitic** Nazi government came to power in Germany in 1933. This was the origin of the state of Israel. Some **migrants** also came from countries where they were not under threat, such as Britain. But most British and American Jews stayed put.

## The Kurds

When the Ottoman Turkish Empire was broken up in 1918, new international borders cut through the area in which the Kurds lived. Some Kurds are in Iraq, some in Turkey, and some in Iran and Syria. They would like to be in a country of their own. This has put them in conflict with the governments of Iraq and Turkey.

## Consider this: diversity

People migrate to escape racial persecution, as many Jews did. Sometimes minorities can create an independent state for themselves, as the Kurds hope to do. But for most minorities it is better to live in peace with a majority which respects their rights. Everyone benefits from diversity.

Saddam Hussein, leader of Iraq until 2003, ruthlessly oppressed the Kurds. In 1991 a Kurdish rebellion failed, and 1.5 million Kurds fled over the mountains to Turkey. They co-operated enthusiastically with the US invasion of Iraq in 2003 and the overthrow of Saddam Hussein. But neither Iraq nor Turkey wants to give the Kurds an independent state of their own.

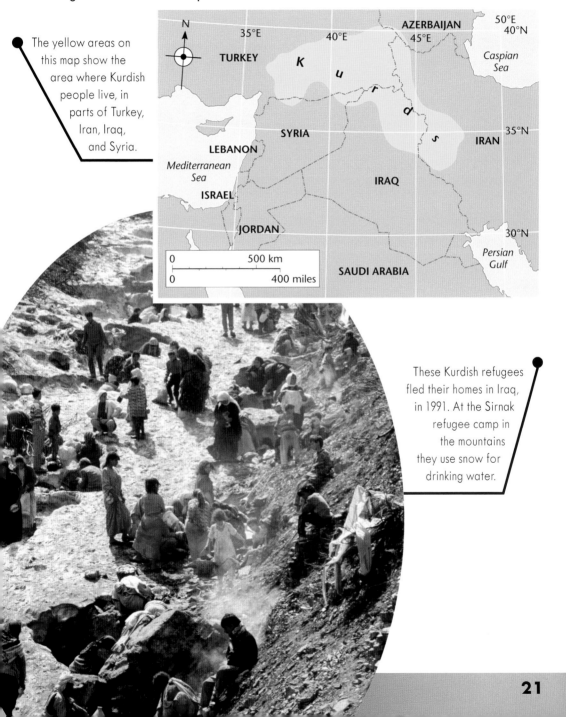

The yellow areas on this map show the area where Kurdish people live, in parts of Turkey, Iran, Iraq, and Syria.

These Kurdish refugees fled their homes in Iraq, in 1991. At the Sirnak refugee camp in the mountains they use snow for drinking water.

# Ethnic cleansing

Sometimes the majority go beyond **persecuting** the minority. They force the minority out of the country altogether, by violence or the threat of violence. This is sometimes known as ethnic cleansing.

## Uganda

Like many other countries in East Africa, Uganda had a small population of Asians. Many of them had small businesses, and were quite prosperous. In 1972 the government expelled them. They gave their businesses and property to Africans who supported the government. Up to 60,000 people had to find a new country. They went to India, Canada, and Britain, which took 28,000. More recently, the government of Uganda has apologized for the expulsion and said that Asians are welcome back. Some have returned to Uganda.

## Cyprus

Cyprus is an island in the eastern Mediterranean. It originally had a Greek population. It was part of the Turkish Empire from 1571 to 1878, and many Turks migrated to the north of the island. It was a British **colony** from 1878 to 1960. After it gained independence in 1960, trouble broke out between the Christian Greeks and the Muslim Turks. Some of the Greek speakers wanted Cyprus to unite with Greece. This would have made the Turkish speakers a tiny minority.

In 1974, a Turkish army invaded the north of the island, which declared itself an independent country. Other countries do not officially recognize this country, because it was created by an illegal invasion. The Greeks were expelled from the Turkish north, and Turks took over their property. The island remains divided. The expelled people are still waiting to return home, or at least be compensated for the property they lost. The **United Nations** is trying to unite the two parts of Cyprus, but both communities must agree with any solution.

## Consider this: reconciliation

Even where ethnic cleansing has happened, communities can live in harmony. Education, understanding, and a positive experience of different cultures all help reconciliation. Most Americans now agree that the treatment of the Native Americans was shameful. They now have more respect for Native American culture.

## Native Americans

In the 19th century, the government of the USA moved Native Americans off their land, to make room for white settlers. Some settlers wanted to kill off the Native Americans. They called them 'animals', 'savages', and 'heathens'. In 1864, 300 Cheyenne and Arapahoe Native Americans were massacred in Colorado. A government report on the massacre recorded that, "Fleeing women, holding up their hands and praying for mercy, were shot down; infants were killed ... men were tortured and mutilated." Not all the settlers thought or behaved like this, and when all the good land had been taken the surviving Native Americans found safety, if little else, in their **reservations**.

## Darfur

Darfur is the western province of Sudan, in Africa. It is inhabited by black Muslim people. They wanted more independence from the Arab Muslim government of Sudan. Some took up arms against the government. In 2004, the government replied by bombing many villages in Darfur. Arab soldiers killed people, looted and burned their villages, and drove them away. Tens of thousands were killed, and 130,000 became refugees in Chad. Over a million people, about 16 per cent of the population of Darfur, were **internally displaced**. They sought safety in the region's towns and in refugee camps. But they were desperately short of food and medicine.

In 2004 these refugees from Darfur are lining up to board trucks to take them to safety over the border in Chad.

**case study:**

# Ethnic cleansing in Yugoslavia

The term ethnic cleansing was first used in the conflicts that followed the collapse of Yugoslavia in the 1990s.

## Yugoslavia

Yugoslavia was formed in 1918, by adding territories from the ruins of the Austro-Hungarian Empire to the independent country of Serbia. These territories were Slovenia, Croatia, and Bosnia-Herzegovina. Much of the area had been part of the Turkish Empire for hundreds of years, and many people had become Muslims, but most people were Christian, either Catholic or Eastern Orthodox. Each state had minorities from other states of Yugoslavia. In Bosnia, there was a mixed population of Catholic Croats, Eastern Orthodox Serbs, and Muslims. There was an Albanian-speaking minority in the part of Serbia called Kosovo, although Albania was an independent neighbouring country.

This map shows the states that made up Yugoslavia between 1918 and 1989.

Yugoslavia held together until it was invaded in 1941 by Germany in World War II. A racist Croat militia, known as the Ustaŝi, tried to wipe out the Serbian minority in Croatia. One estimate is that 700,000 people died. They were mainly Serbs, but also Jews and gypsies.

## Disintegration

Yugoslavia was reunited as a **federal** republic at the end of World War II in 1945. But after 1989, the federation began to fall apart. Slovenia left the federation first, and in 2004 it joined the European Union. Then Croatia, after a brief war, achieved independence. Macedonia became independent in 1991. Bosnia-Herzegovina also left the federation.

# Consider this:
## rebuilding

The conflicts in former Yugoslavia have made this region the poorest in Europe. People are leaving as economic migrants, to join the refugees from war and ethnic cleansing. The region is now being helped by more prosperous countries to rebuild itself, and to keep the peace.

Fighting broke out in Kosovo in 1999. These refugees are crossing into Albania from Kosovo, after a seven day walk from Mitrovice. Serbian government forces fought rebels from the Albanian-speaking population.

## Bosnia

The Croats in Bosnia wanted to unite with Croatia, but the Serbs wanted to stay in the Serb-dominated Yugoslav federation. The Muslims wanted Bosnia to be independent.

In 1992 civil war broke out. The Serbs quickly gained control of over half of the country. They declared an independent Serb republic, and set out to ethnically cleanse it of Croats and Muslims. Muslims and Croats also carried out ethnic cleansing in the areas they controlled. In 1993 the conflict became more complex. Muslims and Serbs formed an alliance against the Croats in Herzegovina. Rival Muslim forces fought each other in north-western Bosnia. Croats and Serbs fought against Muslims in central Bosnia.

## Massacres and intervention

Forces from the **United Nations** created 'safe havens' for Muslim civilians. Three of these were the towns of Sarajevo, Gorazde and Srebrenica. In 1995, Srebrenica was attacked by Bosnian Serb forces, and 7500 Muslim men and boys were killed. Outside countries finally decided to intervene to end the conflict. Countries from **NATO** sent planes to attack Serb positions and so help the Muslims and Croats make big territorial gains. Thousands of Serbs were expelled as a result. The Dayton peace agreement created two territories, one for Bosnian Muslims and Croats, the other for Serbs. An international peacekeeping force went in. Between 1992 and 1995, about 250,000 people died and hundreds of thousands were **displaced**. Many of them have not yet returned home. In 2002, there were 372,000 refugees from Bosnia-Herzegovina living mainly in Serbia, the USA, Sweden, Denmark, and the Netherlands.

# Genocide

Sometimes, the majority or dominant ethnic group goes beyond driving the minority away. The majority attempts to wipe out the minority altogether, by mass killing. This is called **genocide**.

This map shows the Armenian region of Turkey, and the deportation and emigration of Armenians.

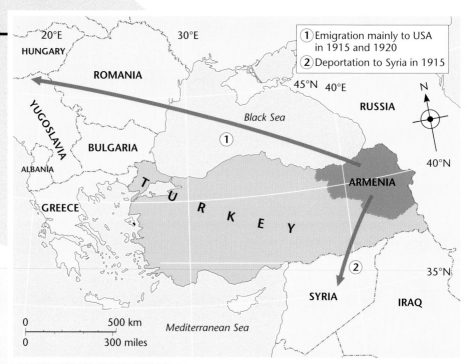

## Turkey and Armenia

In 1915 Turkey was at war with Russia. The Armenian people, who were Christians, lived in both Turkey and Russia. The Turkish government thought the Armenians were co-operating with the Russians, and planning an independent Armenia. The Turks decided to get rid of all the Armenians. Up to three million people were affected. As many as one and a half million may have died in massacres or in **concentration camps** in Syria. Of the survivors, 320,000 emigrated. Turkey was one of the losers in World War I, and the peace treaty of 1920 created an independent Armenia. Turkey invaded, split Armenia with Soviet Russia, and put an end to Armenian independence once and for all. Thousands more died, but some were able to emigrate mainly to the USA. By 1923 there were very few Armenians left, and Turks occupied the empty country.

The eternal flame burns as part of a monument to the victims of the genocide of 1915 in Yerevan, Armenia.

## The Nazis

The Nazi government, led by Adolf Hitler, came to power in Germany in 1933. They believed in the superiority of their **Aryan** race, and hated other races. Hitler decided not just to expel Jews from the country, but to eliminate them. Jews in Germany began to be **persecuted**. They emigrated if they could. Between 1933 and 1939, 270,000 Jews left Germany. Britain accepted Jewish refugees, but limited the number who could go to British-controlled Palestine to 1500 a month. The government of the USA restricted the number of German Jews it allowed in to 75,000 between 1933 and 1941. Hitler wanted to conquer and occupy the countries to the east of Germany. Germany invaded Poland in 1939, and Soviet Russia in 1941. This brought many millions of Jews under their control.

## The Holocaust

The German armed forces in Soviet Russia included special squads which rounded up and killed the Jews in each city the army took. At the same time, Jews from all over German-occupied Europe were sent to camps. In concentration camps, mostly in Poland, they were worked to death. In extermination camps, thousands of victims a day were gassed and cremated. The best known extermination camp is at Auschwitz, in Poland. Jews were not the only victims: 200,000 gypsies were also killed.

As many as six million people, most of them Jews, died in this **holocaust**. Perhaps 65 per cent of all the Jews in German-occupied Europe died. What made the genocide so overwhelming was that for much of the war, Germany controlled almost the whole of Europe, so there were very few places for Jews to escape to.

## Never again

The word genocide was created after World War II, to describe the killing in eastern Europe under German control. The Universal Declaration of Human Rights was part of the reaction to this 'crime against humanity'. It was meant to ensure that genocide would never happen again.

**case study:**

# Genocide in Rwanda

In 1994, an estimated 800,000 people in Rwanda, Africa were killed in just 100 days, because of their race. Two huge waves of refugees fled the country.

This map shows Rwanda and the direction of refugee movements.

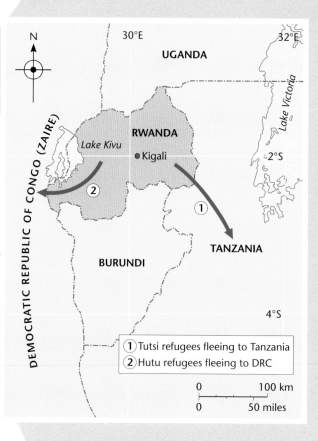

① Tutsi refugees fleeing to Tanzania
② Hutu refugees fleeing to DRC

```
0          100 km
0          50 miles
```

## Hutus and Tutsis

Rwanda has two ethnic groups, the Hutus and the Tutsis. The Hutus are the majority. They speak the same language, live in the same areas, and follow the same traditions. The tension between the two groups increased during the 20th century. In 1916 the region became a **colony** of Belgium. The Belgians treated the Tutsis as superior to the Hutus. They gave them better jobs and education. Resentment among the Hutus gradually built up, until there were riots in 1959. More than 20,000 Tutsis were killed. Many more fled to the neighbouring countries of Burundi, Tanzania, and Uganda. When Rwanda became independent in 1962, the Hutus took over as rulers of the country. Over the next 30 years, the Tutsis were blamed for every problem.

## Rising tension

In the early 1990s, Tutsi refugees in Uganda, supported by some moderate Hutus, formed the Rwandan Patriotic Front (RPF). Their aim was to overthrow the government led by President Juvenal Habyarimana and return to their homeland in safety. Habyarimana accused Tutsis inside Rwanda of being RPF supporters. Unrest between the government and the RPF continued. On 6 April 1994, President Habyarimana was killed when his plane was shot down. This triggered a **genocide.**

Since the age of ten, Théogène Sindikubgabo has had to be father and mother to his younger brother, Jean-Claude. In 1994 both their parents, an older brother, and a sister, were killed. Since then Théogène has supported his little brother, while coping with his own grief.

## Mass murder

In the capital city, Kigali, soldiers murdered the leaders of the political opposition, in revenge for the killing of the president. Almost immediately, the massacre of Tutsis began all over the country. A militia called the Interahamwe was formed, with 30,000 members. Interahamwe, soldiers, and police officers encouraged ordinary citizens to join in the killing. In some cases, Hutu civilians were forced to murder their Tutsi neighbours. Hutus who had the courage to refuse to kill, were killed themselves. Hundreds of thousands of Tutsi families fled into neighbouring countries.

## Peace and justice

In July 1994, the RPF captured the city of Kigali. The government collapsed, the RPF declared a ceasefire, and the killing ended. Up to two million Hutus fled to Zaire (now the Democratic Republic of Congo). These refugees included many who had taken part in the massacres. A new multi-ethnic government was formed. It promised all refugees a safe return to Rwanda.

These refugees from Rwanda are waiting to cross the border into Bukavu in the Democratic Republic of Congo (previously called Zaire).

# Political persecution

In a revolution or civil war, one group of people takes over the government from another. Members of the losing side may be **persecuted** by the winners, and forced to flee for their lives.

## One-party states

In the 20th century, many countries had one-party governments. These were governments made up only of the successful political party, with a strong leader. He demanded total loyalty. To question the leader's policies was seen as treason. It was not even safe to keep quiet. People who had opposed the ruling party in the past, or were of the wrong social class, were in danger. Governments of this sort, who thought they were right in all they did, had little respect for **human rights**.

## China under Mao Tse-Tung

Most of the one-party **regimes** of the 20th century were **communist**. In China, the communists led by Mao Tse-Tung took power in 1949, after a long civil war. The communists were the party of the workers and peasants. When they came to power they killed landlords and gave their land to the peasants. One estimate is that one million landlords were killed.

Mao's policies disrupted life for ordinary people, causing great suffering. In the 1950s, he decided that whole villages, not individuals, would make the decisions about who owned the land and how it should be farmed. In 1958, he tried to industrialize the country overnight. Instead of growing crops, people tried to make iron in their back yards. These huge changes caused chaos. Not enough food was grown and this led to a famine in 1959–1961, in which up to 20 million people may have died. The government then persecuted educated people, and even the children of people who had been in power before the communists. In the 1950s and 1960s, one million refugees escaped from China into Hong Kong (which then belonged to Britain). That may have been as much as 50 per cent of Hong Kong's total population.

This poster shows Mao Tse-Tung applauding as he stands on a platform overlooking the crowds in Bejing, China, in 1971.

In 1973 Henry Kissinger was Secretary of State in the USA. In the 1930s, he was a Jewish refugee from Nazi Germany.

## Cambodia and the Khmer Rouge

Between 1975 and 1979 the Khmer Rouge ruled Cambodia. They were communist. They hated anything which showed the influence of the West or **capitalism**. They forced people to leave the cities and work on the land. All the country's professionals, including doctors and teachers, were killed or sent into hiding. Wearing glasses was seen as a sign of education, and could be punished by death. The Khmer Rouge abolished money and banned religious worship. Thousands of people were tortured, interrogated, and killed.

The Khmer Rouge was driven from power when Vietnam invaded Cambodia in 1979. The Khmer Rouge's rule had created chaos in the countryside, and when the regime collapsed there was a famine. The Khmer Rouge continued to fight the Vietnamese, and then the government of Cambodia, until the late 1990s. This brought more suffering to Cambodia. Thousands of refugees fled into camps on the border with Thailand. They were supported there by the **UNHCR** for many years. Two million people, about 20 per cent of the population of Cambodia, died during the Khmer Rouge years, from either persecution or famine.

# The Soviet Empire, 1917–1991

The **communist** regime in the Soviet Union, also known as the USSR, was the first one-party state of the 20th century. It inflicted terrible suffering on the people it thought were its enemies.

This map shows the 'Iron Curtain', that separated Communist, Soviet-occupied Eastern European countries and the rest of Europe, between 1945 and 1991.

## Revolution and civil war

The communists came to power in Russia in the revolution of 1917. They were soon attacked by forces trying to reverse the revolution, and civil war followed. The civil war lasted until 1921, and created two million refugees. The communists finally won. They formed the government of the Soviet Union, as they now called their country. They thought that they were a unique political and social experiment, which was under threat from the rest of the world. They also feared people inside the country who wanted to reverse the revolution.

## Stalin

Josef Stalin ruled the Soviet Union from 1924 to 1953. Under his rule, the country became a merciless one-party state. Everyone lived in fear of the secret police, which enforced the party's rule and punished its opponents. The party controlled not just what people did but what they read, discussed, and even thought.

## Famine in the Ukraine

The Ukraine was part of the Soviet Union, but it had been independent briefly between 1917 and 1922. Stalin wanted to destroy the Ukraine as an independent nation. In 1932–1933 he imposed a terrible famine on the Ukraine. All food stocks were forcibly taken away. A military boundary was placed around the area to prevent food getting in and people getting out. About seven million people died.

## Gulags

The secret police set up labour camps, or gulags, where people accused of 'crimes against the state' were sent to do hard labour. Many of the camps were in the far north of Russia, or in Siberia. Winter conditions were so harsh there that few prisoners survived. More people died in the Vorkuta group of camps between 1932 and 1957 than died in Auschwitz in World War II (see page 27). At the height of the terror, the camps held up to 13 million people. That was 10 per cent of the country's population.

## Forced migrations

The Soviet Union contained many minority populations. Stalin did not trust them to stay loyal. When Germany invaded the Soviet Union in 1941, he moved all or part of many minority populations to Siberia. They included 40,000 Estonians, 80,000 Latvians, 80,000 Lithuanians, 400,000 Ukrainians, 200,000 Crimea Tartars, 400,000 Volga Germans, and 800,000 Kalmuks.

## Eastern Europe

At the end of World War II, victorious Soviet armies occupied the countries of eastern Europe. The Soviet Union imposed communist one-party regimes on these countries. In 1956, Hungary rebelled. The revolt was put down by Soviet tanks, tens of thousands of people were killed, and by the end of the year 171,000 refugees had fled Hungary. The next country to try to escape the Soviet Empire was Czechoslovakia, in 1968. Once again, Soviet troops occupied the country, but this time with much less bloodshed and far fewer refugees.

## Consider this: the end of the empire

The Communist Party stepped down from power in the Soviet Union between 1989 and 1991. The communist regimes of eastern Europe soon collapsed. Now people were free to leave, but they had less reason to move because they were no longer being persecuted.

In 1956 these Hungarian refugees reach eagerly for food at the Traiskirchen camp, after crossing the border from Hungary. They have fled the Soviet crushing of the Hungarian uprising.

# chapter four

# The issues

## International law and order

We have seen the suffering, and sometimes migration, that can be caused by conflict and **persecution**. What can be done about it? One answer is for international organizations to try to prevent war and defend **human rights**.

### The United Nations

The **United Nations** (UN) was formed in 1945 by the countries that won World War II, led by the Soviet Union, Britain, and the USA. Its aim was to prevent future wars. The UN has not been a total success, because there have been many wars since 1945, but it has tried hard to resolve conflicts and keep the peace. It produced a Universal Declaration of Human Rights (see page 6). This provides the basis for international law and good practice on conflict, oppression, and the rights of refugees.

In 2003 UN soldiers from Uruguay confront a crowd outside the UN headquarters in Bunia, a town in the Democratic Republic of the Congo. The soldiers are there to keep the peace in the country, and stop the ethnic Hema and Lendu militia from attacking civilians.

## Economic sanctions

One way to punish repressive regimes is by applying **economic sanctions**. These prevent trade with, or investment in, a particular country. They helped to bring down the **apartheid** regime in South Africa. But when they were used against Iraq in 1991–2003 they caused misery for the people, without changing the regime.

## UNHCR

The UN appointed the **High Commissioner for Refugees (UNHCR)** and produced the Geneva **Convention** (see page 7). But the UNHCR cannot act alone in caring for refugees. It relies on the governments of countries where there are refugees, and on aid charities.

## The roots of the problem

The UN, its richer and more powerful member countries, and other international organizations, are known together as 'the international community'. Can the international community help to solve some of the problems that lead to war?

- In too many countries, the **regime oppresses** all the people or persecutes some of them. The international community could put pressure on these regimes to behave better.
- Companies that make weapons sell them to regimes that oppress their own people and threaten their neighbours. The international community could control the arms trade more firmly.
- Desperate poverty in developing countries creates tensions which lead to conflict. The international community could do more to help countries escape poverty.

## The Cold War

Between 1945 and 1991, there was a 'Cold War' between the Soviet Union and western nations, led by the USA. The two did not fight each other, but took sides in wars in smaller countries. Instead of trying to make peace, each alliance sought victory for its side. For example, during the civil war in Angola, Africa, the Soviet Union and the USA backed opposing sides.

## The new world order

When the Soviet Union collapsed, the USA remained as the world's greatest power. Has it successfully used its power to stop wars, prevent wars, and remove the roots of war? It launched a war to remove the Taliban from power in Afghanistan, in 2001. It launched another to remove Saddam Hussein from power in Iraq, in 2003. Is this how other oppressive regimes will be dealt with from now on? How else can the world change repressive regimes? Rewards may work better than punishments. For example, many countries want to join the European Union, because of the economic benefits it brings. To be allowed to join, they have to meet high standards on human rights and **democracy**.

# Caring for refugees

How well are refugees and **asylum seekers** treated in the countries to which they flee? It depends on where they come from, where they go to, and how many there are.

## Exiles

Exiles usually get the best treatment. An example of exiles is the white South Africans who opposed the **apartheid** regime and left the country in the 1970s and 1980s. Exiles are often welcomed by the host country. They are few, and they are often educated, intelligent people who can make a useful contribution in their new country. The host country may also allow them to campaign for change in their home country, as exiled South Africans did.

## Post-war Europe

Millions of Germans were forced out of Poland and other east European countries at the end of World War II. Their obvious host country was Germany, within its new borders. West Germany absorbed 12.6 million, and East Germany 4.4 million refugees. They spoke the same language and were of the same nation. West Germany quickly became prosperous enough to provide them with homes and jobs. Britain accepted 160,000 **displaced people**, many of them from eastern Europe. They did not want to return to a homeland that had become part of the Soviet Union.

## Developing countries

Most wars, and most refugees, are now in the developing countries. During the civil war in Afghanistan in the 1980s, there were two million Afghan refugees in Iran and 1.8 million in Pakistan. There were hundreds of thousands of refugees from Cambodia in camps in Thailand between 1979 and 1992. Refugees from Rwanda went to Tanzania and Zaire, two of the poorest countries in the world.

A refugee from war in Cambodia collects her food rations in a refugee camp in Thailand.

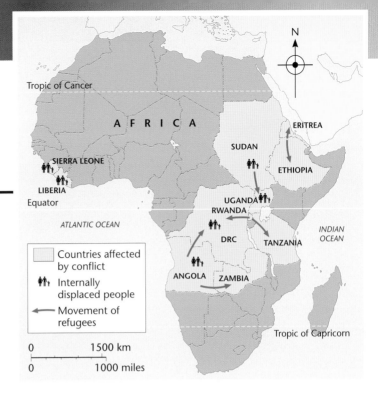

This map shows African countries affected by conflict in the 1990s, including those sheltering refugees from neighbouring countries.

## Problems of cost

These reluctant host countries are poor. If they spend money on the refugees they have less to spend on their own people. Often the local people near the refugee camps will try to help, but they have little to spare. International aid charities have the same dilemma. They, too, have limited budgets. They may have to abandon work with the poor people of the host country, to help the even poorer people in the refugee camps. Sometimes just bringing the conditions in the camps up to acceptable standards of shelter, food and water supply, and **sanitation**, makes the refugees better off than the local people.

## Overlapping conflicts

In 1995 there were about 6.4 million refugees in Africa. That was about 1 per cent of the continent's total population. The countries in which there was conflict made a continuous area from Angola to Sudan. There was another group of war-torn countries in West Africa. People sometimes fled from their own country to a neighbouring country that was also in turmoil. Often the fighting made it impossible for aid to reach the refugees. That was why 3.5 million people died in the Democratic Republic of Congo between 1994 and 2004.

## Consider this: an uncertain welcome

It shows how desperate people are to get away from war and persecution that they will move without knowing what sort of welcome they can expect - if any.

# Are refugees safe?

Sometimes refugees are not safe even when they reach refugee camps. Their **persecutors** may follow them into the camps, or fighting may break out near by.

## Is anywhere safe?

Camps for **internally displaced** people can be as unsafe as anywhere else in a civil war. Bay Kein, a displaced person in Cambodia, had to flee from war several times. "I was born in a village called Traing, and married there in 1968. In the Khmer Rouge times we were forced to move, twice, but when the Vietnamese liberated us in 1979 I returned to Traing. Until 1989 we lived in peace. In 1989 fighting started and we fled to a village called Kok Punlay. Without any land, we worked for other farmers. In 1992 we went to Beng Ampil refugee camp, but in 1993 the camp was attacked and we came here, to Omal village, for safety. In 1994 we went back to Beng Ampil and built a new house. We stayed for six months and then the fighting started again and we came back here, to Omal, and we've been here ever since."

Bay Kein makes a living by weaving mats out of straw at her home in Omal village, Cambodia.

## Pursuit

Even refugee camps in another country are not always safe. They may be especially vulnerable if they are thought to be bases for fighters in the country of origin. The government of Israel thought this about the Palestinian refugee camps, in the countries surrounding Israel. In 1982, members of a Lebanese Christian militia allied to the Israeli army massacred 800 people in the Sabra and Shatila Palestinian refugee camps in Beirut, Lebanon. The Israelis said that the camps were bases for Palestinian terrorists, who had invaded Lebanon.

# Consider this:
## no place like home

Attacks on refugee camps show that the only real security for refugees is when there is peace and they can return home. Until then, they have a right to feel safe from the war they have fled.

This map shows the location of the Hwe Ka Loke refugee camp on the border of Thailand and Myanmar.

[Map showing Southeast Asia with the following labels: CHINA, INDIA, MYANMAR (BURMA), BANGLADESH, THAILAND, LAOS, VIETNAM, CAMBODIA, Bay of Bengal, Gulf of Thailand, Tropic of Cancer, Hwe Ka Loke. Scale: 0–500 km, 0–300 miles. Coordinates: 30°N, 20°N, 10°N, 90°E, 100°E. Compass pointing N.]

## Hwe Ka Loke

Hwe Ka Loke is a refugee camp in Thailand for Karen refugees from neighbouring Myanmar (formerly Burma, see page 6). One of the refugees is Naw Ku, a widow with three children, whose husband was killed by government forces. She brought her family to the camp, hoping that they would be safe. She soon found she was wrong. "The camp leader had had a letter from the government-supported militia, saying that everyone in the camp should go back to Burma or they would burn the camp. The camp leader called a meeting and asked us what we wanted to do. No-one wanted to go back to Burma. Within a few days of that, the militia attacked . . . we woke up the children and ran to the field behind the house, and stayed there the whole night. I saw the flames, but when we got back into the camp I was relieved to find that my house hadn't burned. I never thought I would have to run again when I came here. I don't feel safe now. I'm always wondering if they will come again. I suppose there is some safety in numbers here."

# Desperate migrants

Even if your refugee camp is safe, and the conditions are not too bad, it is still a place you want to get away from as soon as possible. The longer you have been waiting, the more desperate you become. And if you live in a country where you are both poor and **oppressed**, you will also be desperate to leave.

## Long-term refugees

People can be in refugee camps for many years. A World Refugee Year was organized in 1959–1960. Its aim was finally to find homes for the 32,000 refugees who had been in European refugee camps since 1945, and the 915,000 Palestinians who had been in camps since 1948. By the end of the year, there were still 7000 people in European camps, but the camps were finally closed in the early 1960s. The Palestinian camps are still in use. It shows how much worse the world's refugee problem has become, that the numbers from 1959 seem small in comparison with today's figures.

## Destinations

One reason why the Palestinian camps have endured for over 50 years is because the Palestinian leaders, and the governments of the Arab

Thousands of people from Cuba, like these on their raft, have crossed the sea to the USA to escape the poverty and **human rights** abuses of their country.

## Consider this:
### debt, danger, and deportation

Migrants borrow money to pay the smugglers, face danger on the journey, and may finally be caught and returned home. But many are still prepared to take these risks.

countries where the camps are, insist on the Palestinians' "right of return" to Palestine. The refugees are reluctant to settle anywhere else. The European refugees, on the other hand, could not or would not return to homes that were part of the Soviet Union. They moved to new countries. Their favourite destination was the USA.

## A long wait

Sometimes refugees have to wait a long time for peace to come to their home countries. The war in Angola lasted 27 years. Conflicts in Sudan, Colombia (in South America), and Afghanistan have also continued for decades. Even when peace finally comes, the refugees' homeland may be ruined. Roads, railways, water supply, and electricity may all be destroyed. There may be no seeds or tools to grow a crop, no schools or medical care. Tired of waiting, or with no hope of return, people long to start a new life in a safe and prosperous country.

## Poverty and persecution

Even where there is peace, in most developing countries there is poverty and oppression. It is hardly surprising that people try to leave, to find safety and prosperity in Europe or North America.

## Smuggling people

Some people offer to smuggle **migrants** into countries where they want to go. This has become a big business for criminal gangs. The migrants pay a lot of money. Their journey is difficult and dangerous. Migrants are smuggled into Britain in lorries crossing the Channel on ferries from France or Holland. In 2000, 60 Chinese illegal **immigrants** hid in a lorry coming to Britain. The driver closed the air vent of the lorry, and 58 of them suffocated.

Over a million people fled Vietnam after 1975. Many went to Hong Kong, which at that time belonged to Britain.

# The rights of refugees

International law says that countries should take in refugees and people seeking asylum. But what if the people in the host countries do not welcome them? There are strong arguments for and against accepting refugees and **asylum seekers**.

## Human rights

The Geneva **Convention** gives rights to refugees who are fleeing **persecution**. Persecution means that one or more of the rights listed in the **UN** Universal Declaration of Human Rights is being denied (see page 6). The idea of human rights may seem simple, but in practice it can be complicated.

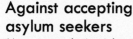

An immigration official checks a truck at the port of Calais, France, before it drives on to the ferry to Dover, England.

## Against accepting asylum seekers

Many people in rich countries are worried about a 'flood' of **immigrants**. They fear that people will be allowed to come in as asylum seekers, even though they do not have a 'well-founded fear of persecution'. Under international law, people should seek asylum in the first country they reach that can provide them with safety. When people seek asylum in a more distant country, it raises doubts about their motives.

Their real motive, some people claim, is **economic**. The **migrants** want to escape poverty and get jobs in rich countries. It is true that some illegal immigrants are pulled by the promise of well-paid work, not pushed by fear. Genuine asylum seekers, who are granted asylum in their new country, often settle down and find work. They are in effect economic migrants, even though this was not their reason to migrate. If they do not find work, they may benefit from **social security**, health services, and education. They have not paid for these things. They are paid for by the people who work, through their taxes.

## In favour of accepting asylum seekers

- The moral view: **Democratic** countries that respect **human rights** have always given refuge to people fleeing from countries where human rights are not respected. We should continue this generous tradition, and in doubtful cases err on the side of the asylum seeker.

- The practical view: In a country with an ageing population, we need economic migrants, especially if they have skills we are short of, or are willing to do low-paid jobs with unsocial hours. If some of the people who are claiming asylum are really here for jobs, it does not matter – we need them and they are welcome.

- The compassionate view: If people are prepared to take the risks of being smuggled here, they must want to be here very much or things must be very bad where they came from. Let them stay.

- The liberal view: When people complain about false asylum seekers and illegal immigrants, what they really fear is people of another race. We should recognize the benefits of a multi-cultural society.

- The internationalist view: Rich countries should help poor countries to escape poverty, and encourage their **regimes** to respect human rights. Then their people would happily stay there.

- The safety view: Sometimes refugees and people still living under **oppression** may blame the richer countries for their problems. They have nothing to lose, and may turn to violence and terrorism against the people they blame for their situation.

In 1991, these refugees were stopped at sea by US officials and sent back to Cuba.

# chapter five

# Conclusion

## Survival and hope

The subject of refugees and **asylum seekers** can be depressing. Some people can be very cruel, and cause great suffering. But people are great survivors, and to survive such problems, to keep going, to hope, to plan, to help each other, is a triumph.

## El Salvador

There was a civil war in El Salvador, Central America, in 1979–1991. Tens of thousands died, and many thousands fled to refugee camps in Honduras. But the war ended, the refugees returned, and the government gave them land. Peace has made development possible.

Baudillo Cruz Dubón describes his experience. "In the 1980s the army moved us away from our communities. They killed people. I sought refuge in Honduras. We were there for seven years. It was like being in gaol in the camp. We had nothing to do. We had food, but around the fence were Honduran soldiers who would arrest us if we tried to leave."

Baudillo and his family returned to El Salvador after the war. They were resettled in a small community called Guarjila. They got land, and help from a local organization, CORDES, to make the most of it. CORDES is supported by Oxfam, an international aid agency.

● Baudillo describes his new life.

"Now I feel that I am the same as when I was at my dad's place and I had banana trees and tomatoes. When we can grow our own food we can at least eat . . . I have received technical assistance, seeds, banana trees, coffee trees, barbed wire, and tools from CORDES. I feel that I am improving now. Before working with CORDES I didn't grow pineapples, bananas, tomatoes, radishes – and now I do. My family has bananas, radishes, and pineapple to eat. I also grow coffee and sweet potatoes. It has improved our diet, and I don't have to buy as much food. We have a good diet and we have plenty to eat, and my children are at school."

Baudillo

## Consider this:
### understanding the issues

Thinking about the ideas and examples in this book should help you to make more sense of news stories about war, persecution, refugees, and asylum seekers. Behind the headlines and issues there are people, on the move, suffering, and surviving.

Angélique with the cow which has improved life for her family in Rwanda.

## Rwanda

Angélique Makamana was just twelve years old when her parents and two older brothers were killed during the **genocide** in Rwanda (see page 28). She found herself responsible for bringing up her four younger brothers and sisters. She managed to keep all the other children in education, but she had to leave school to earn money to feed the family. In 2002 an international aid agency called Send a Cow, gave her a cow. The cow soon calved. Now the family had milk to drink, and surplus milk to sell. Angélique has been able to return to school.

## Cambodia

Vanna lives in Sak Phoy village in Cambodia. She is married and has four children. She describes how the family survive.

"This is my home village. We were in a refugee camp from 1979 to 1993. When we came here, my father gave us this plot, to build our house. UNHCR supported us for the first year with 100 kilograms [220 pounds] of rice every month. Now we make a living from the fruit juice stall in front of the house. We also make cakes to sell on the stall. We rent a plot of riverbank land behind the house 20 metres by 70 metres [73 by 255 feet]. This year we are growing peanuts and garlic. My husband catches fish in the lake, to sell."

Vanna

# Civilian casualties, refugees, and asylum seekers

## Civilian casualties in World War II

Every European country suffered many civilian deaths in World War II. In some cases more civilians died than people in the armed forces.

| Country | Number of civilian deaths | Number of deaths in the armed forces |
|---|---|---|
| Soviet Union | 16,000,000–19,000,000 | 8,000,000–9,000,000 |
| Poland | 5,675,000–7,000,000 | 123,178 |
| Yugoslavia | 1,200,000 | 305,000 |
| Germany | 780,000 | 3,500,000 |
| France | 350,000 | 213,324 |
| Greece | 325,000 | 88,300 |
| Hungary | 290,000 | 200,000 |
| Czechoslovakia | 215,000 | 10,000 |
| Netherlands | 200,000 | 7900 |
| Romania | 200,000 | 300,000 |
| Italy | 152,941 | 242,232 |
| Britain | 92,673 | 264,443 |
| Belgium | 76,000 | 12,000 |
| Bulgaria | 10,000 | 10,000 |
| Norway | 7000 | 3000 |
| Denmark | 2000 | 1800 |
| Finland | 2000 | 82,000 |
| Total (estimate) | 27,077,614 | 14,362,177 |

In contrast, Australia lost 33,826 in the armed forces, and the USA lost 290,000, but neither country suffered civilian deaths.

## Refugees, asylum seekers, and internally displaced people

This is the estimated number of people of concern to the **UNHCR**, of 1 January 2004.

| Region | Number of people |
|---|---|
| Asia | 6,200,000 |
| Europe | 4,200,000 |
| Africa | 4,300,000 |
| North America | 978,000 |
| Latin America and Caribbean | 1,300,000 |
| Oceania | 74,400 |
| Total | 17,052,400 |

This total was made up of:

| | | | |
|---|---|---|---|
| Refugees | 9,700,000 | **Internally displaced persons** | 4,400,000 |
| **Asylum seekers** | 985,000 | Others | 912,000 |
| Returned refugees | 1,100,000 | | |

These figures show where the major refugee populations in 2003 had come from, and where they were living.

| Country of origin | Main countries of asylum | Number of refugees |
|---|---|---|
| Former Palestine | Gaza Strip, West Bank, Syria, Lebanon, | 3,000,000 |
| Afghanistan | Pakistan, Iran, Turkmenistan, Russia, India | 2,500.000 |
| Sudan | Uganda, Chad, Ethiopia, DRC, Kenya, Central African Republic | 600,000 |
| Myanmar | Thailand, Bangladesh, India, Malaysia | 586,000 |
| DRC | Tanzania, Congo, Zambia, Burundi, Rwanda | 440,000 |
| Liberia | Guinea, Cote d'Ivoire, Sierra Leone, Ghana | 384,000 |
| Burundi | Tanzania, Democratic Republic of Congo | 355,000 |
| Angola | Zambia, Democratic Republic of Congo, Namibia, South Africa | 323,000 |
| Vietnam | China, USA | 307,200 |
| Iraq | Iran, Kuwait, Jordan, Syria | 280,600 |

These figures show the number of asylum applications submitted in selected industrialized countries, in 2004.

| Country of asylum (population in millions) | Main countries of origin of applicants for asylum | Number of asylum applications |
|---|---|---|
| France (59) | Turkey, Algeria, China, Democratic Republic of Congo, Serbia-Montenegro, Russian Fed. | 61,600 |
| USA (288) | China, Mexico, Colombia, Haiti, India, Venezuela, Cameroon, Ethiopia | 52,360 |
| UK | Somalia, Iran, China, Zimbabwe, Turkey, DRC | 40,200 |
| Germany (82) | Turkey, Serbia-Montenegro, Russian Fed., Vietnam, Iran, Azerbaijan | 35,610 |
| Canada (31) | Colombia, Mexico, China, Sri Lanka, Costa Rica | 25,500 |
| Austria (8) | Russian Fed., Serbia-Montenegro, Nigeria, India, Turkey, Pakistan, Afghanistan | 24,680 |
| Sweden (9) | Serbia-Montenegro, Somalia, Iraq, Albania, Iraq, Russian Fed., Bosnia-Herzegovina | 23,160 |
| Belgium (10) | Democratic Republic of Congo, Russian Fed., Serbia-Montenegro, Slovakia, Turkey, Guinea | 15,360 |
| Switzerland (7) | Serbia-Montenegro, Turkey, Iraq, Georgia, Bosnia-Herzegovina, Algeria, Somalia, Russian Fed. | 14,250 |
| Netherlands (16) | Iraq, Somalia, Afghanistan, Iran, Burundi | 9,780 |
| Norway (4) | Afhanistan, Russian Fed., Serbia-Montenegro, Somalia, Iraq, Iran, Nigeria, Turkey | 7,950 |
| Ireland (4) | Nigeria, DRC, Romania, Somalia, Sudan, China | 4,770 |

In 2003–2004 Australia accepted 11,700 refugees and asylum seekers.

These figures show the countries with large populations of internally displaced people, on 1 February 2005.

| Country | Number of internally displaced people |
|---|---|
| Sudan | 5,300,000–6,700,000 |
| Columbia | 1,575,000–3,410,000 |
| Democ. Repub. Congo | 2,300,000 |
| Uganda | 1,400,000 |
| Iraq | over 1,000,000 |
| Algeria | 1,000,000 |
| India | 600,000 |
| Indonesia | 600,000 |
| Azerbaijan | 575,000 |
| Myanmar | 526,000 |

These are the ten countries from which people made the most asylum applications to Britain, in January–March 2004.

| Country | Number of asylum applications |
|---|---|
| Somalia | 1000 |
| Iran | 725 |
| China | 615 |
| Zimbabwe | 545 |
| Turkey | 460 |
| Democratic Republic of Congo | 405 |
| Pakistan | 405 |
| India | 385 |
| Iraq | 340 |
| Afghanistan | 285 |

# The world of refugees map

In the early years of the 21st century, many countries created or took in refugees. Some other countries had internally-displaced people as a result of wars.

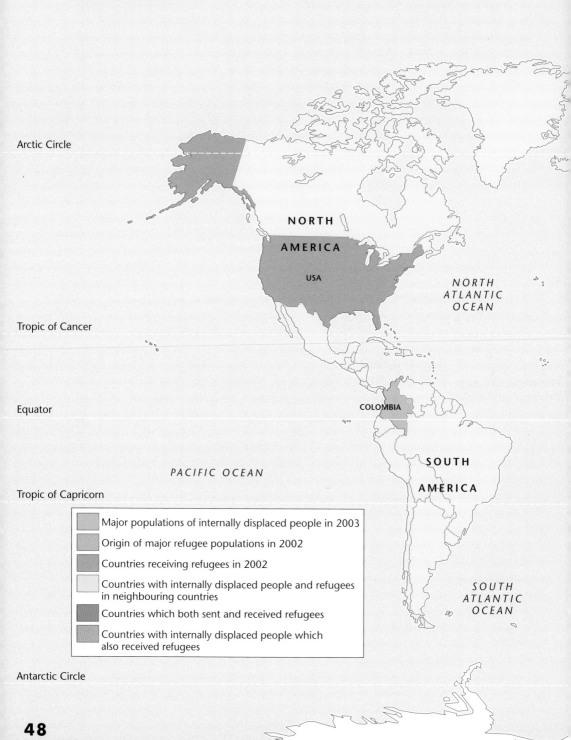

Arctic Circle

NORTH

AMERICA

USA

NORTH ATLANTIC OCEAN

Tropic of Cancer

Equator

COLOMBIA

SOUTH

AMERICA

PACIFIC OCEAN

Tropic of Capricorn

Major populations of internally displaced people in 2003

Origin of major refugee populations in 2002

Countries receiving refugees in 2002

Countries with internally displaced people and refugees in neighbouring countries

Countries which both sent and received refugees

Countries with internally displaced people which also received refugees

SOUTH ATLANTIC OCEAN

Antarctic Circle

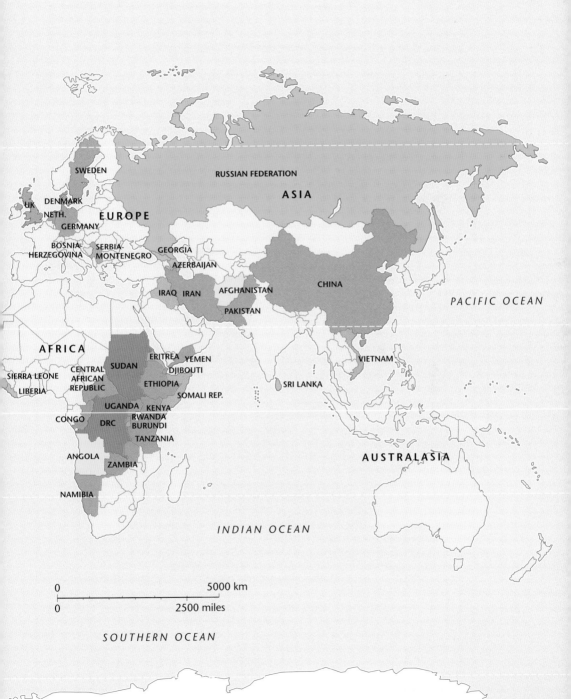

SWEDEN

UK
DENMARK
NETH.
GERMANY

EUROPE

RUSSIAN FEDERATION

ASIA

BOSNIA-
HERZEGOVINA
SERBIA-
MONTENEGRO

GEORGIA

AZERBAIJAN

IRAQ    IRAN

AFGHANISTAN

CHINA

PACIFIC OCEAN

PAKISTAN

AFRICA

ERITREA    YEMEN

SIERRA LEONE

CENTRAL
AFRICAN
REPUBLIC
SUDAN

DJIBOUTI

ETHIOPIA

VIETNAM

LIBERIA

SOMALI REP.

SRI LANKA

UGANDA    KENYA

CONGO
DRC
RWANDA
BURUNDI

ANGOLA

TANZANIA

AUSTRALASIA

ZAMBIA

NAMIBIA

INDIAN OCEAN

0                    5000 km

0            2500 miles

SOUTHERN OCEAN

ANTARCTICA

**49**

# Timeline of key events

| | |
|---|---|
| **1492** | Spain expels its Jews |
| **1502** | Spain expels its Muslims, called Moors |
| **1562–1598** | French wars of religion |
| **1618–1648** | Thirty Years War in Europe, sparked by religious differences |
| **1620** | first Puritans leave England for the USA |
| **1685** | Huguenots leave France for England |
| **1831–1832** | in the USA Native Americans are expelled from Georgia and moved to Oklahoma |
| **1848** | in Europe several revolutions fail and revolutionary exiles flee to Britain |
| **1881** | in Russia the attacks against the Jews begin and Jews flee to Britain and the USA |
| **1914–1918** | World War I: total military deaths in European nations are 8,427,015 |
| **1915** | in Turkey there is **genocide** of Armenians |
| **1917–1921** | Russian Revolution, followed by civil war. A Norwegian called Fridtjof Nansen sets up the Nansen Relief organization to help Russia's two million refugees. |
| **1918** | The district of Sub-Carpathian Ruthenia, in Central Europe, taken over by Ukraine from the Austrian Empire |
| **1919** | Sub-Carpathian Ruthenia becomes part of Czechoslovakia |
| **1920–1922** | Turkish-Greek war: 1,350,000 Greeks leave Turkey and 430,000 Turks leave Greece |
| **1933** | the Nazi party comes to power in Germany. Over the next six years, 270,000 Jews leave Germany to escape **persecution**. |
| **1936–1939** | Spanish Civil War |
| **1939** | Sub-Carpathian Ruthenia taken over by Hungary |
| **1939–1945** | World War II: in Europe over 27 million civilians and 14 million armed forces are killed. By the end of the war there are 12 million **displaced people**. |

| | |
|---|---|
| **1945** | Sub-Carpathian Ruthenia taken over by the USSR |
| **1947** | India is granted independence. In the partition that follows 500,000 people die and 17 million are forced to migrate. |
| **1948** | the **United Nations** Universal Declaration of Human Rights |
| **1948** | the state of Israel is created, leading to the first Arab-Israeli war and the start of the Palestinian refugee problem |
| **1949** | Geneva **Convention** on the treatment of prisoners of war |
| **1951** | Geneva Convention on the rights of refugees |
| **1956** | revolution in Hungary is suppressed by Soviet forces and 171,000 refugees flee to Austria |
| **1967** | in the Third Arab-Israeli war Israel occupies the West Bank and Gaza Strip |
| **1975** | Angola gains independence and a civil war begins |
| **1975–1979** | under the Khmer Rouge **regime** in Cambodia two million people die |
| **1979** | start of civil war in Afghanistan |
| **1991** | First Gulf War against Iraq. Saddam Hussein of Iraq crushes a Kurdish rebellion and 3.5 million Kurds flee to Turkey. |
| | Sub-Carpathian Ruthenia becomes part of the independent Ukraine |
| **1992–95** | war in Bosnia-Herzegovina |
| **1994** | in a genocide in Rwanda one million people die and two million become refugees |
| **2002** | end of civil war in Angola |
| **2003** | there are more than 17 million refugees, returned refugees, internally displaced people, and **asylum seekers** in the world |
| **2004** | attacks on the people of Darfur in Sudan force hundreds of thousands into refugee camps over the border in Chad, and over one million into internal displacement |

# Glossary

**anti-personnel mine** explosive device designed to be set off by a person walking over it

**anti-Semitism** feeling hatred for Jewish people

**apartheid** government policy in South Africa until 1991, of keeping black and white people apart and denying civil rights to black people

**Aryan** in the beliefs of the German Nazi party, the Aryan races, including the Germans and other northern Europeans, were superior to other races

**asylum seeker** someone who wants to live in a country other than the one they were born in, because they fear persecution in their home country, because of their race, religion, or opinions

**atrocity** cruel act, such as torture or execution, carried out against a large number of people, often during war

**capitalist** a free-market economy in which property is held by individuals

**civil rights** a person's rights as a citizen, for example to a vote in elections, to fair trial, to hold an opinion, and to join organizations

**colony** a country ruled by the government of another, more powerful, country

**communist** an economy in which all property belongs to the state. Communist parties want to introduce such an economy. Communist countries have this kind of economy.

**concentration camp** prison used by the governments of one-party states to punish their opponents

**Convention** document setting out international rules, for example on the treatment of refugees, which countries are expected to follow

**democracy** a country whose government is chosen by free and fair elections. In a democracy human and civil rights are usually respected.

**discrimination** unfavourable treatment of an individual or a group of people, because of their race, religion, language, or other reason

**displaced person** someone who has had to move away from their homes, usually because of war

**economy/economic** a country's economy is created by the work people do, the money they spend, and the goods and services they produce

**evacuation** in war, governments may organize the evacuation of civilians from areas where they are in danger from bombing or other attack

**federal** form of government in which power is shared between a central, national government, and the states that make up the country. The USA and Germany have federal forms of government.

**genocide** mass killing of one ethnic group, usually the minority in a particular country, by another group, usually the majority

**ghetto** part of a town or city in which a particular minority, especially the Jewish community, live, often because they are forced to stay there

**guerrilla**  a fighter who is not a member of the official armed forces. Guerrillas do not wear uniform, and often carry out hit-and-run raids, rather than fighting pitched battles.

**holocaust**  the murder of millions of Jews by the Nazis during World War II

**human rights**  basic rights of all human beings – civil rights, plus the right to necessities such as food, shelter, health care, and safety

**immigrant**  person who has migrated into a country

**internally displaced person** someone who has fled from their home to escape fighting, but has not crossed a border into another country

**malnourished**  suffering from an inadequate diet. This can mean not enough food, or food lacking things essential for good health, like protein or vitamins.

**Middle Ages**  in European history, the period between the 11th and 15th centuries

**migrant**  person who has moved from one country to another, or from one part of a country to another, usually permanently

**NATO**  North Atlantic Treaty Organization, a military alliance including the USA and many western European countries

**oppression**  oppressive regimes deny the civil and human rights of some or all of their people

**persecution**  attacks on people ranging from the denial of civil rights to physical assault, abduction, imprisonment, or murder

**regime**  the government in power in a particular country, or the kind of government, for instance democratic or one-party

**requisition**  to take food, fuel, or shelter from civilians, without payment, and whether the civilians are willing or not

**reservation**  area set aside for a group of people to live in, especially for Native Americans in the USA

**sanctions**  governments sometimes apply sanctions against other countries whose regime they disapprove of. Economic sanctions include cutting off all or part of the trade and investment between the two countries.

**sanitation**  safe, clean ways of dealing with human waste

**sect**  subdivision of one of the main religions. Islam has two main sects, Sunni and Shia. Christianity has Roman Catholics, Lutherans, Calvinists, Eastern Orthodox, and many more sects.

**social security**  money benefits paid to people by the state, for example unemployment benefit

**sub-continent**  region smaller than a continent but containing several countries. The Indian sub-continent contains India, Pakistan, Bangladesh, and Sri Lanka.

**UN**  United Nations: set up in 1945 to prevent war and encourage international co-operation

**UNHCR**  United Nations High Commissioner for Refugees: set up in 1950 to protect refugees and resolve refugee problems worldwide

# Further resources

## A place to visit

Beth Shalom Holocaust Centre
Laxton
Newark
Nottinghamshire
NG22 0PA
www.holocaustcentre.net

## Websites

Amnesty International campaigns on behalf of people who are persecuted for their beliefs:
www.amnesty.org.uk

The International Committee of the Red Cross looks after victims of conflict – prisoners of war and refugees:
www.icrc.org/eng

International aid agencies look after refugees and internally displaced people:
www.oxfam.org.uk
www.christian-aid.org.uk
www.savethechildren.org.uk

United Nations High Commissioner for Refugees:
www.unhcr.ch

The full text of the UN Universal Declaration of Human Rights:
www.un.org/Overview/rights.html

A reference guide to the Geneva Conventions:
www.genevaconventions.org

The Campaign to End Genocide:
www.endgenocide.org

The Minority Rights Group campaigns on behalf of racial, religious, and language minorities:
www.minorityrights.org

The Refugee Council works with, and campaigns for the rights of, refugees and asylum seekers:
www.refugeecouncil.org.uk

Worldaware works in the UK to raise awareness of international development issues:
www.worldaware.org.uk

Anti-Slavery International campaigns against slavery in the modern world:
www.antislavery.org
www.stophumantraffic.org

These organizations help refugees and asylum seekers in Australia

www.immi.gov.au
Department of Immigration and Multicultural and Indigenous Affairs in
Australia

www.immigration.museum.vic.gov.au
Website for the Immigration Museum in Melbourne, Australia

www.refugeecouncil.org.au

www.amnesty.org.au

## Further reading

Connolly, Sean, *Troubled World: United Nations – Keeping the Peace,*
(Heinemann Library, 2003)

Cooper, Adrian, *Just the Facts: Racism,* (Heinemann Library, 2003)

Dave, Dalton, *People on the Move: Nomads and Travellers,*
(Heinemann Library, 2006)

Downing, David, *Troubled World: Conflict: India and Pakistan,*
(Heinemann Library, 2003)

Downing, David, *Troubled World: Africa: Postcolonial Conflict,*
(Heinemann Library, 2003)

Gifford, Clive, *World Issues: Refugees/Racism,*
(Chrysalis/Belitha Press, 2002

Hepplewhite, Peter, *World in Flames: Civilians,* (Pan Macmillan, 2001)

Horrell, Sarah, *The History of Immigration: Immigrants from Eastern Europe*
(Franklin Watts, 2002)

Nusbacher, Ayreh, *Just the Facts: War and Conflict,*
(Heinemann Library, 2003)

Shuter, Jane, *The Aftermath of the Holocaust,*
(Heinemann Library, 2003)

Stewart, Ross, *Witness to History: The Arab-Israeli Conflict,*
(Heinemann Library, 2004)

Taylor, David, *Troubled World: The Wars of Former Yugoslavia,*
(Raintree, 2003)

Zephaniah, Benjamin, *Refugee Boy,* (Bloomsbury, 2001)

# Index